THE LIVING LANDSCAPE

Discovering the Critical Zone

Eric Parrish
Suzanne Anderson

Essex, Connecticut

Welcome to the Living

An imprint of Globe Pequot, the trade division of
The Rowman & Littlefield Publishing Group, Inc.
4501 Forbes Blvd., Ste. 200
Lanham, MD 20706
www.rowman.com

www.MuddyBootsBooks.com

Distributed by NATIONAL BOOK NETWORK

British Library Cataloguing in Publication Information available

Library of Congress Cataloging-in-Publication Data available

ISBN 978-1-63076-396-1 (cloth)
ISBN 978-1-63076-397-8 (epub)

Printed in Mumbai, India
April 2022

Air

Life

Soil

Water

Rock

Landscape

Earth is a rocky planet,
and yet it is full of life.

*All life on Earth can be found
in a thin, outer layer called…*

THE CRITICAL ZONE!

Earth's surface layer
between the treetops and
the bedrock teems with
life and pulses with water.

Why Is It the Critical Zone?

The critical zone is the ever-changing skin of the Earth. Here air, water, animals, plants, soil, and rock interact.

Each part affects the others.

Everything needed for life comes from interactions in the critical zone. Life resources include the food we eat and the water we drink.

Humans live within the critical zone. Everything we do, including a hike in the mountains, is connected to the critical zone.

Where Is All the Rock?

Earth's rock is often hidden under soil and plants. Why?
Rock breaks down when exposed to rain, snow, and air. Small
rock fragments mix with plant remains to build soil. Microbes and
animals in the ground get in the soil-making act too.

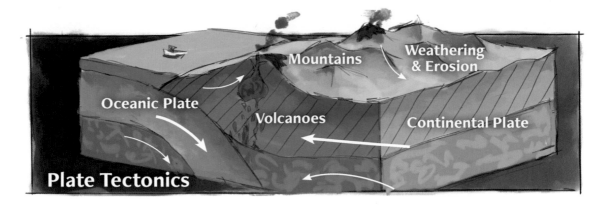

Plate tectonics forces drive collisions of massive plates to build mountains. Mountains are a good place to see bedrock. On the steep slopes, soil erodes faster than it is made from rock.

Over time, rock becomes soil by
- weathering (rocks breaking apart)
- erosion (removal of rock and soil)

These processes are helped by
- water, ice, and air
- plants
- animals (even humans!) and microbes

Always Changing

Every year, every day, every hour, and every minute, the critical zone changes.

Some changes occur slowly, like soil forming from rock, or even more slowly, like mountain building. Some changes occur quickly, like wildfires and mudslides.

Trees bring about change in the critical zone. Over its life, a tree sends out roots and grows, drawing important nutrients from the soil and rock. When a tree dies, it may fall over, exposing its roots and sometimes yanking out solid rock! The tree helps build the soil in which it lives.

Did You Know?

Scientists measure changes. They gauge sediment carried in streams, measure ground movements with lasers and satellites, and analyze changes in soil and rock.

The Skin of the Earth?

Soil is like the planet's skin. It is organized in layers, called horizons.

Soil is a mixture of small rock particles and decaying (dead) plants. Soil has lots of pore spaces (holes) that make homes for living things, both big and small.

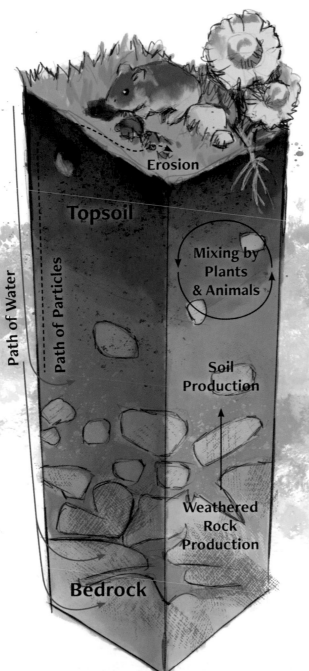

Erosion

Topsoil

Path of Water

Path of Particles

Mixing by Plants & Animals

Soil Production

Weathered Rock Production

Bedrock

Organic: A layer of mostly dead plant leaves. Plants and animals mix this organic material into the topsoil layer.

Topsoil: A nutrient-rich layer of both organic material and minerals from rocks. This is a good place for plants to root and other organisms to live.

Saprolite: A layer with more rock fragments and fewer plant roots. This is where rock weathers into soil particles with help from plants, microbes, fungi, and even burrowing animals!

Soil Is the Crossroads

Soil forms where the air (atmosphere), rock (lithosphere), water (hydrosphere), and living things (biosphere) all meet.

In this crossroads, water moves, minerals change, gases are produced, and life thrives.

Parts of Soil

Particles
- minerals
- rock fragments
- organic matter

Microbes
- bacteria
- fungi
- protozoa

Air Pockets

Did You Know . . . ?

Microbes are so small that 1 teaspoon of soil can contain up to one billion (1,000,000,000!) microbes. There are many kinds of microbes, and each performs a different task. Some are producers, some are consumers, and some are decomposers. Soil is also home to bigger organisms like centipedes, beetles, and other insects.

Important Functions of Soil

1. Soil absorbs, stores, and releases water.

2. Soil anchors plants and provides nutrients they need to grow.

3. Soil impacts the atmosphere by releasing and absorbing gases.

4. Soil is a habitat for organisms, such as tiny microbes or bigger animals like mice.

Meet . . . the Warty Microbe?!?!

One of the many microbes found in mountain soils is called verrucomicrobia (ver-ru-co-mi-cro-bi-a).

The name means "wart"! This microbe gets its name from the wartlike structures biologists see on the microbe under a microscope.

Mighty Microbes

Microbes are the tiniest organisms in soil, yet they play big roles in the critical zone.

Even though they are invisible to the human eye, their impact can be seen.

Microbes break down organic matter (dead plants), release nutrients from rocks, and can turn nitrogen in air into forms plants can use. They drive the chemical engine of the critical zone.

Verrucomicrobia

Did You Know . . . ?

Carbon and nitrogen are key ingredients for life. Carbon atoms are basic building blocks of living cells, while nitrogen atoms are essential for growth and reproduction.

Movers and Shakers of the Critical Zone

Microbes are important, but there are bigger animals like ants, worms, and even gophers that impact the critical zone. They are important digging and tilling machines in the soil.

In the mountains, gophers move huge amounts of soil and rock.

They move this material up, down, and all around as they nest, eat, and explore underground. Their digging helps turn rock into soil and slowly plows meadow soils.

Skull with Teeth

Incisors and Cheek Pockets

Meet . . . the Northern Pocket Gopher!

The northern pocket gopher is well-suited for life underground. It has a strong, sturdy body; small eyes; and short limbs.

This rodent has impressive front digging claws and long and continuously growing teeth called incisors. Its incisors help the gopher gnaw its way through soil to find roots to eat.

Most important, the pocket gopher has pouches in its cheeks that close. This allows the gopher to dig without getting dirt in its mouth!

Long Front Digging Claws

Life Above the Ground

Trees, plants, and even mushrooms growing aboveground are all connected to the soil below. They draw nutrients, water, and support from the soil, groundwater, and rock below.

Plants provide food and habitats for insects, birds, and animals. In turn, these creatures live, eat, reproduce, and die within the critical zone.

Animals Aboveground Shape the Critical Zone

Elk scrape the ground with their hooves. Bears dig holes to find tasty grubs. Beavers change rivers by building dams and lodges. All animals poop! Their poop, also called scat, returns important nutrients to the soil!

Did You Know . . . ?
One-third of all freshwater on Earth is stored below our feet as groundwater.

Water in the Ground

Water moves through the critical zone as part of the water cycle. Water from snowmelt and rain soaks into soil. Some is used by plants, some drains into streams, and some seeps into groundwater. All the water flows back to the ocean to start the cycle again.

Water is key to life. Plants, animals, and microbes all need water.

Water drives erosion. Rivers move water and sediment from mountains to lowlands and the sea.

Water in the critical zone keeps rivers flowing and plants growing!

Mountain Runoff

Glacier

Lake

Creek in the City

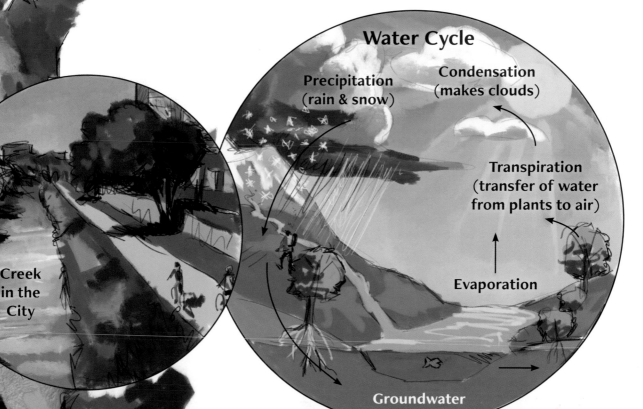

Water Cycle

Precipitation (rain & snow)

Condensation (makes clouds)

Transpiration (transfer of water from plants to air)

Evaporation

Groundwater

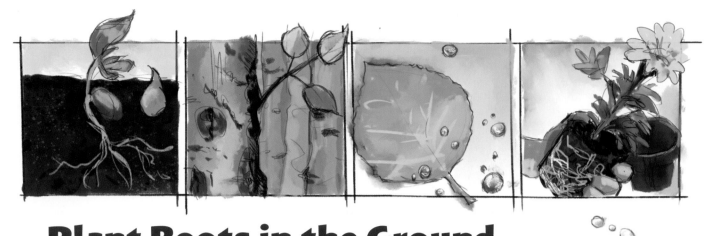

Plant Roots in the Ground

Plant roots grow down into the soil so that plant leaves can reach up toward the sky.

Plant roots absorb water. The water flows up to leaves to help the plant grow. Then, the water evaporates out into the air.

Roots both cause and prevent erosion. Falling trees yank up rocks. But roots also hold soil together, slowing erosion.

Did You Know . . . ?

The deepest tree roots scientists have found reach 225 feet down, more than the height of twelve giraffes!

Tree roots are as different as the environments where they grow.

Trees in wet climates tend to have shallow roots, while trees in dry climates may have a deep "tap root" to reach groundwater even during droughts.

Wet Climates

Dry Climates

Did You Know . . . ?
On average, plants return over half of all rainwater to the atmosphere.

Life from Light!

Plants, including trees, make their own food. They use raw materials from the critical zone and a process called photosynthesis.

During photosynthesis, plants convert energy from the Sun into chemical energy that makes it possible for plants to grow.

Trees from Thin Air?

In photosynthesis, trees use atoms from air, water, and rock to build the cells of their leaves, branches, and roots.

Along the way, they break oxygen atoms out of water molecules, making the air we breathe.

In essence, the tree grows from air and water, with a dash of rock!

Water

Sunlight

Oxygen

Carbon Dioxide

Cycles, Cycles, Cycles

Water is on the move. Carbon is on the move. Even fragments of rock are on the move in the critical zone. These movements drive interlocking cycles of water, carbon, and rock. The cycles renew and sustain the environment that supports life.

Carbon

What Are Those Cycles?

- *Water cycle*: Water moves from the ocean, to the atmosphere, to the ground, and back again. Along the way, water keeps plants growing and rivers flowing.

- *Carbon cycle*: Carbon atoms move from the atmosphere, to plants, to soil and rock, and back again. Along the way, carbon builds plants and trees, and fuels animals and people.

- *Rock cycle*: Rock is pushed up to build mountains and is torn down by erosion. Along the way, rock makes soil and provides nutrients for plants.

These cycles connect. Flowing water erodes rock. Newly eroded rock fragments make soils that nurture plants. Plants and trees move water from the ground back into the atmosphere.

Without these cycles, Earth would be a very different planet.

What Is the Critical Zone?

Scientists study the critical zone. They find that rock, soil, water, plants, and air are all connected, and all of these parts depend on each other.

Humans are part of this vast system, and we need to understand how all the systems work and how we fit in.

Earth is a rocky planet that supports abundant life. This life is confined to a shallow layer called the critical zone. Here, rock, soil, air, water, and living organisms interact.

By studying the critical zone, we help ensure that life on Earth continues to survive, grow, and thrive.

SUN

MERCURY

VENUS

EARTH

MARS

JUPITER
(one of four
gas giants)

Asteroids

A ROCKY PLANET

Eight planets and thousands of smaller objects, including asteroids, comets, and dwarf plants, orbit the Sun. Earth is one of the four rocky planets (Mercury, Venus, Earth, and Mars) closest to the Sun. Next comes the asteroid belt, composed of thousands of fragments of rock left over from solar system formation. Farther from the Sun are the four gas giant planets—Jupiter, Saturn, Uranus, and Neptune.

The rocky planets have iron cores surrounded by silicate rock. The gas giants are made of mostly hydrogen and helium, which makes them light for their size.

Learn more: https://spaceplace.nasa.gov/menu/solar-system/

OR WATER PLANET?

Earth is the only planet with abundant water in all its states—water, ice, and vapor. Only a small fraction (2.5 percent) is freshwater, and it is constantly cycling through the critical zone.

Plants are important in the water cycle. Roots draw in rainwater that soaks into the soil. The water is pulled, like juice in a straw, up to the leaves. Some water is used for photosynthesis, but most of it evaporates out of tiny holes in leaves called stomata. Why would a plant lose water this way? Plants use stomata to take in the carbon dioxide they need to grow. Water loss is the cost of photosynthesis.

Learn more: https://kids.kiddle.co/Stomata,
https://www.usgs.gov/special-topic/water-science-school

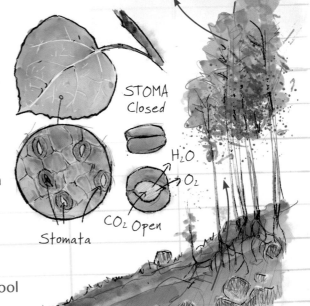

BREATHE!

Leaves return water to the atmosphere.

STOMA
Closed

H_2O

O_2

CO_2 Open

Stomata

Roots draw in slow-moving groundwater.

MAKING SOIL

Turning solid rock into soil takes time. The speed depends on the kind of rock, the rainfall and temperature, and what plants are present.

It can take as long as 20,000 years to make 1 inch of soil, or as little as 20 years. A soil column may represent many thousands of years of development. Soil is an important resource that takes a long time to replace.

Learn more: https://www.soils.org/about-soils, https://www.soils.org/iys/monthly-videos/

This soil profile is at least 15,000 years old.

LIFE

Clumps Contain

Aggregates store nutrients that plants use.

Fungi

Organic

Water

Sand & Clay

Microbes

SOIL AGGREGATES: A HELPING HAND

Have you ever held a soil clod? They usually break down between your fingers into small clumps called soil aggregates. Each aggregate is a loosely glued together cluster of the particles in a soil. Aggregates protect organic matter, hold air, and help water movement.

Learn more: https://www.ndsu.edu/soilhealth/soil-health/soil-property-1/aggregation/

Stable aggregates are important to a healthy soil!

ROCK + WATER + SOIL = LIFE
(This Is Why It's Critical!)

Acknowledgments

The authors thank researchers associated with the Boulder Creek Critical Zone Observatory, the Dynamic Water Critical Zone project, and the Denver Museum of Nature & Science departments of zoology and photo archives for input on this project, and the National Science Foundation (grant 1331828) for support. Early educational reviewers H. Ragsdale, B. Roddiger, D. Morgan, K. Krause, K. Kross, J. D. Loughlin, R. Loughlin, and E. Carpenter, provided valuable feedback. Finally, the authors express their gratitude to Vienna Fontaine and her family for their inspiration, and to Ellen Sukovich Parrish for her extensive support.

This book is targeted for grades 3–6.

About Critical Zone Science

A geologist named Gail Ashley first proposed the idea that scientists should study the Earth's surface as a cohesive system from bedrock to treetops. She called this system the critical zone. Since 2007, the US National Science Foundation has funded critical zone science and research. They established critical zone observatories (CZOs) to bring together scientists to build a new understanding of processes in the critical zone. Eventually, ten CZOs were established. Each observatory benefited from cross-disciplinary collaboration: experts working together from fields spanning hydrology, geochemistry, geomorphology, ecology, and geophysics. Together the CZOs worked to understand critical zone structure, how it evolves, and how it would respond to changing natural and human-altered conditions.

In 2020, NSF transitioned from CZOs to a new Critical Zone Collaborative Network. They selected nine thematic clusters, each focused on a different science topic, and a network coordinating office. The thematic clusters build on the legacies of the CZOs and extend their spatial reach. They address new scientific questions such as the effects of urbanization, the role of dust in sustaining ecosystems, processes in deep bedrock that affect critical zone evolution, the aftermath of disturbances such as fire and flooding, and changes in coastal areas related to rising sea level.

Critical zone research will help scientists predict how the critical zone orchestrates "ecosystem services"—like freshwater—and also provide new information about how natural and human systems are linked. These answers are crucial to determine the availability of life-sustaining resources, including food and drinking water, that affect our planet's habitability.

More information and opportunities to learn about critical zone science and research can be found at: https://criticalzone.org/.